D1540398

Rogério Andrade Barbosa

African Animal Tales

AFRICAN ANIMAL TALES

Rogério Andrade Barbosa

Illustrations by Ciça Fittipaldi
English language adaptation by Feliz Guthrie

VOLCANO
· PRESS ·

Volcano, California

English language edition first published in 1993 by Volcano Press, Inc.

First published in the Portuguese language in 1987 with the title BICHOS DA
ÁFRICA: LENDAS E FÁBULAS
Illustrated by Ciça Fittipaldi
© 1987 Rogério Andrade Barbosa
© 1987 Comp. Melhoramentos de São Paulo, Indústrias de Papel
Caixa Postal 8120 - São Paulo - Brasil

Library of Congress Cataloging-in-Publication Data

Barbosa, Rogério Andrade.
   [Bichos da África. English]
  African animal tales: legends and fables / Rogério Andrade Barbosa;
adapted by Feliz Guthrie; illustrations, Ciça Fittipaldi.
     p. cm.
   Contents: The considerate fly -- The tortoise and the leopard -- The
serpent's bride -- The raingod's vengeance -- The cassolo bird and the
bee -- Why dogs sniff each other -- The cunning of the tortoise -- The
tortoise and the jackal -- The hawk and the eagle -- The cat and the rat.
    ISBN 0-912078-96-0: $17.95
    1. Tales--Africa. 2. Animals--folklore. [1. Folklore--Africa. 2.
Animals--Folklore.] I. Guthrie, Feliz. II. Fittipaldi, Ciça, ill.
III. Title
PZ8. 1.B2334Af 1993   92-42378
398.24'5'096--dc20   CIP
                                     AC

Books may be ordered directly from Volcano Press, P.O. Box 270, Volcano, CA
95689 USA. Telephone: (209) 296-3445, FAX (209) 296-4515. Please call, write or
fax for ordering details.

Printed in Brazil.

AFRICAN ANIMAL TALES

TABLE OF CONTENTS

1. The Considerate Fly

It was a hot, sunny day, toward the end of the dry season. Dust and flies and shimmering heat made the children complain. "My feet are burning!" grumbled one.

"Do you remember what happened this time last year?" asked her older brother. "The men went to the fields that weren't cleared for planting yet, and set fire to the brush before the coming rains made it too wet to burn. But then, a terrible wind arose, sweeping the flames through the stubble, into the jungle and driving all the animals across the plains."

"Did it drive away the flies?" demanded another child, swiping an impatient blow at one that buzzed around her head.

The older brother laughed. "Don't you know the story of the considerate fly?"

"The considerate fly!" all the children exclaimed. "How could a fly be considerate?"

"I will tell you," said the older brother.

One day, a big black Fly was buzzing around, and she happened to land on the top log of a pile of firewood. This particular log was smooth and slick, so the Fly skidded along it and skated right up to... a snake, coiled among the logs to sleep. With a loud buzz, the Fly woke the snake. "Madame Serpent!" she cried. "You must not sleep here! Men will come to fetch this firewood, and if they see you, I wouldn't give much for your chances!"

Quickly, the snake slithered down over the logs and into a dark, round hole in the ground just the right size for her. But she was met by a loud squeal of fear... there was a mouse in the hole. When he saw the snake, he froze with

terror. The next moment, he was streaking for his burrow's back door. He ran in such a panic that he dashed out right between the legs of a pheasant who was strutting by. The pheasant started shrieking, too. The noise woke up a monkey who had just dozed off on a tree branch overhead.

Confused by the shrill cries, the monkey was even more startled when the pheasant came whirring up at him from the ground below. The monkey jumped so that the branch broke, and he fell... right onto the head of a passing elephant!

Well, of course, the elephant was surprised. She shambled off at a great rate, smashing brush and trampling grass. Unfortunately, the elephant also squashed the nest of a *ntietie* bird, and this bird doesn't put up with much nonsense.

Rocketing out of the grass, she darted this way and that, furious at having her nest destroyed. The *ntietie* has flaming red feathers, and in her blind anger, the bird began to set fire to the grass. The poor elephant didn't know what to do or where to go. She lowered her huge ears as if to beg the bird's forgiveness.

But the chain of misfortunes didn't end there. A passing buck burned his feet in the flaming grass, and he ran to the river to quench the pain. He was in such a hurry, he forgot he was supposed to call out a warning so that the maidens from the village who were bathing in the water could jump out and put

their clothes on. The result was that several of the maidens scarcely had time to cover themselves. Shocked and angry, they bustled off to complain to the chief of their village.

The chief got so mad when he heard what the buck had done, he sent for the unfortunate animal and demanded an explanation. The buck instantly blamed the *ntietie* bird for setting fire to the grass. So the chief sent for the bird.

The *ntietie* blamed the elephant for smashing her nest. The elephant blamed the monkey for falling on her head. The monkey blamed the pheasant; the pheasant blamed the mouse; the mouse blamed the snake. And the snake blamed the Fly.

The Fly felt very small before the angry chief. She looked around for someone else to blame. But there was no one else. Heaving a sigh, she admitted her guilt: "It is true I have been the cause of a large number of mishaps and misfortunes. All I can say is that I was trying to help Madame Serpent. Surely my intentions must count for something!"

Well, the old men of the village put their heads together over the problem. They weighed the good against the bad and decided that the Fly was indeed innocent. And so, they pardoned her.

And yet, there she still is--the ungrateful little nuisance--buzzing around our ears and making us lose our patience with her as much as ever!

2. The Tortoise and the Leopard

The children were excited about the great hunter who had passed through their village that morning. What impressed them most was the number of amulets that decorated his body and his spear shaft.

"When I grow up, I'm going to be a great hunter like that!" one of them declared.

His uncle overheard him. "If you are," his uncle said, "you will have to learn a lot. A great hunter has to know how to build traps that will fool the animals he wants to catch. Animals are clever. It isn't so easy to hunt them as you may suppose."

"Oh, tell us a story about making traps!" the boy cried. The rest of the children joined in. "Yes, tell us a story! Tell us a story!"

This is what their uncle told them:

Old Dame Tortoise, preoccupied as usual by her own thoughts, was rollicking home one day. That is, she was lumbering along under her shell at a sprightlier pace than usual. But she wasn't getting anywhere fast because she kept turning from the path to sniff a wild flower here, or nip off a tender bud there. She should have been paying closer attention to other, more important things. For instance, on the trail in front of her was a large mat of palm leaves. A grass snake wound its slim body across the mat making the dry fronds rustle. Without a second thought, the tortoise followed, when all of a sudden the trail fell away beneath her in a shower of palm leaves and dry sticks. Whump! She landed at the bottom of a deep hole that the hunters of the nearby village had dug in the middle of the path.

Thanks to her tough shell, the tortoise wasn't hurt. But how was she going to get out of the hole? She knew she had to find a way to escape before morning, or she would end up in some villager's soup pot.

Old Dame Tortoise rested her chin on the collar of her shell and thought

hard. She was still thinking when... Swoosh! Thud!... company arrived! It was a magnificent Leopard, long and languid and supple... and fierce. His growl said plainly that he wasn't pleased by the hunters' trick to trap him.

Old Dame Tortoise can think a lot faster than she can walk. Before the Leopard had even noticed that she was in the hole with him, she rasped out in a snooty voice, talking through her beaked nose, "Just what do you think you're doing? Who taught you your manners? Don't you know any better than to barge into a lady's house? Uninvited, too!"

The Leopard whirled around and stared at her in amazement.

"Don't you know I never receive visitors after nightfall?" the Tortoise went on. "Get out of this hole, you uncouth, spotted hooligan!"

This was more than the Leopard cared to take from so ugly and ungainly an old lady. With a coughing snarl, he swiped a blow at the Tortoise, scooping her up and launching her skyward as easily as a child might toss up a smooth pebble. "Get out of this hole yourself, you wrinkled-necked old gourd full of

bones!" he called up after her. "I do what I please!"

"My thanks, Great One," replied the Tortoise softly from where she had landed on the edge of the hole. "I suggest you save your strength for when the hunters come tomorrow. Good night!"

Old Dame Tortoise crawled off for home, relieved and grateful for the chance that had saved her life, but a little smug, too, because of how well she had used that chance to escape from both the hunters and the Leopard.

3. The Serpent's Bride

A wedding brought out all the finery of the village. Every man, woman and child put on the most beautiful and splendid garments they had. There was feasting and singing and story-telling. One elegant guest from a faraway place told the story of a very strange marriage.

Long ago, there was a beautiful maiden who said over and over that she would not marry any young man her father might choose for her. Once when she said it, it was overheard by ears it was not intended for: a Snake was coiled among the branches of a tree above her head.

The words sparked an idea in the Serpent's brain. Sliding down from his hiding place, he raced off through the long grass to the river and away to his cave, far upstream. There he turned himself into a strong and handsome young man. His magic wasn't perfect. He had trouble with his tail which wouldn't disappear properly--even the splendid clothes he put on didn't hide it. But he found that if he walked sideways, he could keep it from showing so much.

When he'd practiced a little, he returned to the village to strut before the eyes of the beautiful maiden. She took one look and fell in love right up to her eyebrows. Catching him by the hand, she tugged him after her and showed him to her startled father. *This* was the husband for *her,* she said. She would marry this man and no other. Her father looked the suitor over with a critical eye. There was something sinister about this young man, he thought, but there was no way to convince his daughter of it. Reluctantly, he agreed to the marriage.

After the wedding festivities, the young couple journeyed to the Snake's cave. There, the bride's radiance and joy soon faded. The poor girl was forced to spend her days cleaning her husband's den, which was a horrible, stinking mess. She tried several times to escape back to her village, but the Snake wouldn't let her.

He kept a guard dog, a guard cat, and a guard rooster. If anybody came near, or if the young bride took a step out of the cave, the dog would bark, the cat would yowl, and the rooster would crow its head off.

But luckily for the bride, she had four brave brothers. One of them was a Seer, one was a Hunter, one was a Carpenter, and the other was a Thief. One night, the Seer had a dream in which he saw clearly that his sister had actually

married a Serpent in disguise and that she was forced to work for him like a slave.

When the Seer told his three brothers about it, they decided to rescue their sister. Guided by the Seer, they journeyed up the green river to the cave of the Snake. The brother who was a Thief now took his turn. He brought out meat and fish and corn which he had stolen in the village. The dog took one sniff of the meat and forgot to bark. The cat pounced on the fish and forgot to yowl. And the rooster couldn't crow with his beak full of corn. Thief, Seer, Carpenter and Hunter burst into the Serpent's cave together. "Come, sister, quickly! Don't even stop to smile at us! Come, run!"

Like a gazelle, she dashed to the river bank. But, oh! To their horror, the canoe was destroyed! The Serpent, creator of all evil arts, had known the brothers were coming and had lain in wait. The moment they left their boat, the Snake had smashed it to pieces.

So now, it was the Carpenter's turn. Quick as a wink, he built a new

boat from the broken parts of the old one. In another moment, they were paddling for home with their sister in the bow. Looking back, she saw the Snake was after them, swimming so fast the green waters of the river churned and boiled, making it hard for the brothers to steer the canoe.

The Hunter sprang up in the stern with his lance to kill the Snake, but the terrible creature sprouted seven more heads, and the Hunter couldn't tell which one to aim at. "Help me, brother!" he cried to the Seer. "Which is the real head?"

"The second one! That one! There!"

The Hunter's aim was true. His strength was tremendous. With his heart full of love for his sister, he launched his lance at the monster. "Swish!" It hissed through the air. "Thwap!" It drove right through the true head of the Serpent. Writhing horribly, the monster sank below the surface of the river. "Glub... glub... gloop." Slowly, the waters calmed. The Snake was dead.

Rejoicing, the four brothers brought their grateful sister home. She never fell in love again. She preferred to keep house for her brothers because they truly loved her and cared about what happened to her.

4. The Rain God's Vengeance

Malafi was overjoyed. His father had promised that he could go with him to the river to hunt for hippos. All Malafi's little friends were green with envy because it isn't every day somebody hunts an enormous animal like that. This was more than an ordinary hunt--it was a special event. It meant the people of the village would have meat in their pots for a long, long time.

After cutting off the animal's head--a prized trophy for the victorious hunters--they wore their knives down cutting the hippo into bits and pieces.

Since Malafi's envious friends didn't get to go on the hunt, they did the next best thing: they went to Grandfather Ussumane and asked him to tell them a story about a hippopotamus.

This was how the old man answered:

There was a time when hippos lived only on land and shared the pastures with the cattle. But since the hippos were so big, they got most of the grass. The cattle were left with the trampled stubble.

Ugubane, the God of Land and Fire, decided to take the matter in hand because he felt sorry for the cattle. In a storm of dust and smoke, he roared off to complain to Eraga, God of the Rain, who favored the hippos. The God of Land and Fire made no bones about his business:

"Enough of this nonsense, O Powerful Eraga!" he said. "My poor cattle are dying of starvation in the wake of your greedy hippos. You need to do something. Put those overgrown pigs on a diet or teach them some consideration for others."

Offended by his tone, the Rain God answered stiffly: "O Powerful Ugubane, return with your Fire to your Land. From this day forward, the hippopotamus shall live only in the rivers and streams."

But the Rain God muttered something else to himself after Ugubane was gone. He knew a way to teach the God of Land and Fire a few manners in diplomacy. As God of the Rain, Eraga had control of every drop that fell. And he saw to it that not a single drop fell on the Land that Ugubane ruled. A terrible drought scorched the fields and pastures; all the vegetation shriveled and dried in the blazing sun. Hunger and thirst consumed the poor cattle.

They died with their skins stretched like transparent parchment over their hollow bellies.

The God of Land and Fire watched them with outrage and pity in his heart. He knew what he must do to help the cattle. Swallowing his fiery pride, Ugubane went to visit the God of Rain a second time. He bowed before him humbly and waited for Eraga to bid him rise before he spoke.

"O Powerful God of Rain!" Ugubane said. "I see that you are stronger than I can ever be. But I beg for your mercy. The plants are all dry and my cattle are dying."

The proud Rain God swelled up still more when he saw his rival brought to his knees. But the Rain God gave his word--and kept it--that the rains would return to fields and pastures.

However, just in case the God of Land and Fire might win the next time (with gods, you never know!), the hippos decided to come out of the river only at night to feed in the lush, new pastures. Under the cover of darkness, Ugubane was not so likely to notice.

5. The Cassolo Bird and the Bee

The children had spent the day eating honey which they had scraped out of a wild bees' nest, and now they were all sticky and stuffed to bursting. They had found the bees' hiding place in the hollow cavity of an ancient tree growing beside the river. They had a bird to thank for it: with its shrill cries, the *Cassolo* bird had led the children there.

Evening came, and some of the happy children were still singing the bird's praises: "Lion, leopard, swift and strong, *Cassolo* bird is never wrong!"

At bedtime, Malafi's sister asked their mother, "Why does the *Cassolo* make such a ruckus when it finds a bees' nest?"

Here is what their mother said:

Long ago, the *Cassolo* bird and the Bee were good friends. They spent a lot of time together, and each believed the other to be the best friend she could ever have. Each would have given her life for the other--or so they said. But promises have a way of being put to the test.

One day, the only child of the Bee got very sick. The Bee went to the local witch doctor and asked for help. This strange old magician took out three small bones and tossed them into the air. He read the pattern they made when they fell to the ground. "Bee," he said, "your child will live, but only if you make medicine from a feather of the *Cassolo* bird."

The Bee gave the witch doctor a jug of golden honey in payment, and buzzed off to find her friend. "Oh, my dear *Cassolo*," she cried out. "I need one of your feathers in order to save the life of my only child!"

"Of course, Friend Bee," replied the bird at once. "Dry your tears."

She plucked a long, lovely feather from her tail and gave it to the Bee. Sure enough, it saved the life of the Bee's child.

It wasn't long afterward that the only child of the *Cassolo* bird suddenly fell ill. And since there weren't very many witch doctors in the neighborhood, the bird went to consult the same one who had helped the Bee. The old magician told her that her child's life would be saved if she made some medicine from a bee's wing.

The *Cassolo* paid the witch doctor with a jug of palm-tree wine and flew off to her friend with a tranquil heart; she was certain that her friend would help to save her child's life.

But the Bee answered, "My dear *Cassolo*, if I had as many wings as you have feathers, I'd sing you a different tune. But I have only four wings, and I need all four to fly. I am deeply sorry, but I cannot give you one."

The desperate *Cassolo* went to another hive for help. But none of the bees would sacrifice a wing to save the little bird's life. At last, embittered and

grieving, the *Cassolo* said to herself, "If the Bee is my friend, who are my enemies?" And ever since that day, the *Cassolo* has made it her business to reveal the bees' nests to honey thieves so that all their hard work to make combs of golden honey would be lost.

*   *   *   *

"Did the *Cassolo's* only son die, then?" cried Malafi's sister in distress.

"No, no, no!" her mother said quickly, dismissing that problem with a wave of her hand. "The *Cassolo* found another way to save her son."

"She did? But what about the witch doctor's prediction?"

"Witch doctors have their own reasons for saying what they say. Now, off to bed with you!"

6. Why Dogs Sniff Each Other

Grandfather Ussumane always liked to tell the children about the glory of the African kingdoms before the arrival of White Man.

One day, Grandfather was going on and on about the great power of the Black rulers in the olden days, when all at once two little dogs ran between him and the children, scattering sparks from the council fire and interrupting his talk.

"Grandfather," Malafi said, taking advantage of the pause to change the subject, "why do dogs always go around sniffing each other?"

"Ah! That is a very ancient story," replied Grandfather.

35

Back in the days when dogs governed themselves, there were two big kingdoms ruled over by two powerful kings. In spite of being rivals, they lived peaceably until one of the kings met the sister of the other. Crazy in love, this king journeyed to his rival's realm.

"Most noble friend," the suitor said, "I came all this long way to ask you for your sister's hand in marriage." He bowed to indicate the lady who lay beside her brother's throne, watching a court jester's juggling.

"My sister! Marry a cur like you?" the rival king barked in fury. "Never! Get out! And don't come back!"

The rejected king went home growling to his court, angry and offended. As soon as he got there, he called a council of war. But the council advised him to give his enemy fair warning, so he sent for his most faithful servant and told him to take a message to the rival king.

"Tell him I mean to come back for another kind of visit! Tell him that I'll attack with all my army and destroy him."

The messenger bowed. "Yes, your Majesty. Is there a message for the lady?"

"No!" growled the king. "But you can tell her brother I don't want to marry any dog that's related to him!"

"Yes, your Majesty." The servant bowed again and went off to prepare for his journey. Just as he was leaving, one of the king's counselors called to him.

"Wait! Stop! You can't go like that! Do you want his Majesty's enemy to think we are all dirty dogs? Look at you! Your paws and your tail are filthy." So, under the orders of the king's counselor, the messenger was thoroughly washed and dried and brushed. They even scented his tail with the most exotic perfumes of the kingdom.

Ready at last for his mission of war, the messenger started off on his journey. The day was bright and breezy, the sun shone bravely, and the birds sang as he trotted along. All washed and brushed and perfumed, the messenger felt better than he could remember feeling in his life. And he began to get an idea.

"I have never smelled so good, or looked so fine," he said to himself.

"What's to keep me from looking for a wife of my own? The king's quarrel is not my quarrel. I don't care if he can't marry his rival's sister. I think I'll visit someone I know: the prettiest she-dog in all of Africa!"

Quick as the wag of a dog's tail, the messenger left the path and trotted off on his own. And *that's* why all dogs go around smelling each other's tails... they're still trying to track down that runaway messenger!

7. The Cunning of the Tortoise

Grandfather Ussumane was a *griot*, one of those special old men who serve an entire region as a living history book. As a young man, he had traveled extensively; he was known and welcomed everywhere.

Grandfather Ussumane was also one of the judges of the local tribunal, since he was famous for his wide experience with all sorts of problems and disputes.

But it was the strange case of the Old Tortoise that the children liked to hear the most--though it was a Lion, and not Grandfather Ussumane, who had been the judge then.

Once there was an old, old lady Tortoise living in the jungle. She was so slow and so old, she had a hard time getting enough to eat. Finally, she asked her neighbor, the Jackrabbit, if he would dig a tunnel for her. "Start it in my burrow and dig all the way to that clearing in the jungle where the animals have their weekly market," she said. "Bring the tunnel up right under the fruit stand."

The Jackrabbit laughed. "You want your own private route? What's the matter? Did somebody trip over you last week on your way to market?"

"Certainly," he added more kindly. "I'll dig you a tunnel." And he did.

The Tortoise thanked the Jackrabbit again and again so that when the tunnel was finished, he went off feeling he had really done a good deed.

The next day, which was market day, the Tortoise crawled through her tunnel. Popping her head out of the hole, she saw all the animals of the jungle selling and buying food: heaps of fruit and bushels of vegetables and mountains of grain. There was a hullabaloo of voices and shouts and grunts and squeals as they bargained and haggled over prices.

The Tortoise drew in a deep breath. With all her might, she shouted, "Hunters! Spears! Arrows! Run! Here come the hunters!" Then she pulled her head back into the hole.

The other animals froze for a moment in surprise. The warning had

come right out of the ground! They thought one of the gods of the jungle had spoken to them. Wild with fear, they dropped everything and dashed in all directions to get away.

The Old Tortoise waited until the clearing was empty and silent. Then she crawled out. Slowly, she filled a big sack with all the food she could stuff into it. She ate better that night than she had in years.

Every market day, she tried the same trick. It always worked. But after a few weeks, the other animals got together and went to see the Lion, the King of the Jungle.

"Your Majesty," said the Monkey, who was their spokesperson, "we can't go on like this. Every market day, we are warned by a mysterious voice that the

hunters are coming. We all drop everything and run. When we get back, most of the food is gone. Can't you do something?"

The Lion thought for a while. "Climb up into the branches at the edge of the clearing," he told the Monkey. "From there you may be able to spot the rascal who's responsible."

The Monkey took the Lion's advice. The next time the strange voice cried out in warning and all the animals ran away, the Monkey stayed right where he was. He was almost too scared to hang on in case the warning wasn't a fake, but he made himself sit still. Then, he saw the Tortoise come lumbering out from under the fruit stand to fill a big sack with the best of everything that could be stuffed into it.

As soon as the Tortoise had bumped back down out of sight, the Monkey scampered off to tell the King of the Jungle what he had seen. The Lion thought it over carefully. Then he sent the Monkey to tell the Tortoise that she must come to be judged. Old as she was, the Tortoise was still a thief, and thieves must be punished.

The Tortoise listened to the Monkey's angry chatter without showing any sign that it worried her. "You have to come before the King tomorrow!" spluttered the Monkey.

"I'll be there," replied the Tortoise calmly.

The next day, when the Tortoise came, she brought a guitar with her. Before the trial could begin, she started to play the lovely instrument. The music was so marvelous that the whole court was soon singing and dancing. Everybody forgot all about the market and the stolen food and punishment for the thief. They danced and laughed and sang and wore themselves out completely. Eventually, they all went home for supper. They had never had such a wonderful time.

After the others were gone, the King said to the Tortoise, "I'd like to have an instrument like yours. Can you make me one as fine as this?"

"Well, it wouldn't be easy," the Tortoise replied with a slow, sly smile. "I'd need a special material to make it with."

"I can get anything you need for it," said the Lion. "I'm the King, after all. No one can deny me what I ask for."

"Fine," said the Old Tortoise. "To make the strings for a guitar like this one, I need stretched monkey gut. Can you get that for me?"

"Of course!" said the Lion. "I'll send the Leopard to catch the Monkey right now. He's probably not far away."

In fact, the Monkey was right overhead, and he heard what the Lion said. Before the Leopard could even be told, that Monkey was swinging through the trees and gone. He never came back.

Since the Monkey was the only witness to the crime, there was no one left to accuse the Tortoise. She was never punished. But there was no more warning voice at the weekly market, either. The burrow of the Tortoise was stuffed with enough food to last her for a long, long time.

8. The Tortoise and the Jackal

All day long, the village had been in a state of excitement over the wrestling match which took place every year. Only the best wrestlers of the neighboring towns could compete. They rubbed their bodies with oils to keep evil spirits away, and they wore *gri-gris* (protective charms) tied around their arms and legs. The wrestlers began their bouts by kneeling in front of each other. With lightning movements of their hands, they tried to gain advantage by strategic holds on each other. Then they would try to throw each other to the ground. After the bouts ended, there was dancing.

But since this was mainly a festive occasion for adults, the children grew bored. They went to see if one of the old grandmothers of the village had something good for them to eat, and of course, she did. While they ate, she told them about another kind of contest, a wrestling match of wits that took place long ago:

There was once a king who had such a beautiful daughter that all the men wanted to marry her. By night and by day the suitors arrived, some from distant places, all of them laden with expensive gifts for the lovely girl. But the king had already decided that he would give his daughter in marriage to the one who could face the most difficult challenge.

It took several months to narrow them down to a pair of final contestants: the Tortoise and the Jackal.

The king didn't know what sort of new task to set for them; he had almost run out of ideas. The Tortoise, begging permission, made a suggestion:

"To help you choose which one of us is the bravest, let's see who can swallow the most scalding gruel."

The king liked this idea. The Jackal was a little hesitant, but he agreed, also.

Very early the next day the whole village sat down in a huge circle to watch this last contest. The king, his wife and his daughter, all wearing their most colorful robes, sat in the shade of a majestic tree. Eagerly, the people called for the contest to begin, and began to bet on the outcome. Some were for the Tortoise; others were for the Jackal.

At last, the great moment arrived. The two contestants advanced to stand before the king. He rose and signaled for silence. "Which of you wants to be first?" he asked.

The Tortoise, taking a step forward, answered quickly, "I do, Your Majesty!"

The Jackal drew a sigh of relief. He hadn't wanted to be first.

Next, all attention centered on the village cook. Since the night before, he had been tending an enormous pot of boiling corn meal gruel on a big cooking fire. Now, he took up a long-handled wooden spoon and plunged it into the pot. Hot steam rose from the gruel as he filled a gourd with a dollop of corn meal and handed it to the Tortoise.

The Tortoise received it carefully and said to the gathering, "So that no one here will doubt my valor, I will pass this gourd in front of each one of you. Thus, you will see that this gruel is truly boiling." He showed the steaming gourd first to the king, to the queen and to her daughter. Then he showed it to every person of the multitude: the men and the women, the girls and the boys. When he had finished, the gruel was only lukewarm. The Tortoise had no trouble gulping it down in a single swallow to the wild applause of the crowd.

"Jackal," said the king, "now it is your turn."

The brave rival was shaking so much with fear that when he received the scalding gruel, he spilled it on the ground and burned his feet. Howling with pain, he ran away, hopping from foot to foot as he went, followed by the jeering calls of the villagers.

And that is how the Tortoise came to marry the king's daughter.

9. The Hawk and the Eagle

Grandfather Ussumane always seemed to know everything before he was told. So, of course, he knew exactly why all the children were sad that night. During the day, they had made a game of inventing animal traps, and they hadn't watched the cattle as closely as they should have. As a result, two valuable cows had died from eating poisonous plants.

"You're sorry about the cows," Grandfather Ussumane said. "And you should be! The cattle are our greatest possession. We can't afford to lose them just because of a children's game. Let me tell you a little story about someone else who shirked his duty."

Years ago, more years than anyone can count, there lived an Eagle who owned a lot of cattle. One day, he had to make an important journey, so he put the herd in the care of his nephew, the Hawk. During the morning, the Hawk left the herd just to say hello to a friend that he hadn't seen for a week. When he got back, the whole herd was gone! He looked everywhere for them, but they seemed to have been wiped off the face of the earth! Ashamed of himself and afraid of what the Eagle might do, it took all the Hawk's nerve to confess to his uncle what had happened.

"What do you mean, the herd is gone!" the Eagle screamed at his trembling nephew. "We're going to find those cattle right now--you'd better hope so, anyway!"

They started out together, the Hawk trailing the Eagle respectfully, taking care to keep out of reach. They hadn't gone far when they met the Sun, who was resting serenely on a hilltop.

"O Glorious Sun!" called the Eagle. "Sun, who by day sees all things upon the Earth! Can you tell me who has stolen my cattle?"

"Of course," replied the Sun, rising politely. "It was the Moon."

The Eagle and the Hawk flew off to the House of the Moon. "We have come to retrieve the cattle you have stolen!" shrieked the Eagle.

The Moon, beautiful and glamorous, but with a face as cold as stone, showed no sign of remorse. "Ah, yes... your cattle. What a pity. I've already eaten half of them. The other half I sold to the Stars. The only thing I can give you in return are these five coins of gold." Her voice was cool and sweet and soft as night. "Take these coins and buy yourself another herd, my friend."

The Eagle accepted the coins. He gave them to his nephew to carry. "Here. Now don't lose them before we get home. Do you hear me?"

"You can count on me, Uncle!" the Hawk declared, squaring his shoulders. "I'll keep them safe among my feathers."

But as they flew, the wind blew the coins out of his wings. So, when the

two birds arrived home, the coins were gone. "Uncle? Um... Uncle Eagle? I... I lost the.. er, coins."

"Fool that I am!" screamed the Eagle. "Why did I entrust such a treasure to a feather-head like you?" The Eagle prowled up and down with his wings folded behind his back while he cursed his own judgment and his nephew's incompetence. "Well, grumbling won't get the coins back," he decided at last. "They must have dropped down somewhere. We'll go through the whole forest and ask the other birds to help find them."

But they searched in vain. If any of the coins were ever found, no bird confessed to it. Finally, the angry Eagle declared war on all the birds of the earth until his lost coins should be returned to him.

And that is why birds scratch the ground so earnestly: they're still looking for those Coins of Discord. And that's also why roosters call to each other at dawn: one cry means, "Any coins been found, yet?" And the other answers, "Not yet! Not yet! Not-not-not... yet!"

10. The Cat and the Rat

The first rain of the season fell on the village. It rained all day without stopping. It came down in sheets and buckets. The storm had started the night before. The children couldn't remember ever having seen such lightning bolts shoot across the sky. And the thunder! It crashed and roared over the village all night. In the morning, the villagers had to clean out the mud that had oozed into their huts. Others went out to round up the cattle that had broken out of the corrals in terror of the thunder and lightning.

By nightfall, the rain dwindled to a steady, gentle drizzle, perfect weather for story-telling. The children sat inside the warm cocoon of their blankets and listened while their mother spoke softly. "Did you know that Cats and Rats used to be friends?" she said. "They were, you know! What made them stop being friends was a great flood. The rivers overflowed their banks, and everything was washed away."

It seems that in those days, the Cat and the Rat were cultivating more than friendship. They were out tending a field of *cassava* together when suddenly it began to rain. How it did rain! The two friends were lucky to reach high ground before the river overflowed and left them stranded on a hilltop that had suddenly become an island.

"How are we ever going to get back to the village?" the Cat wondered aloud.

"Maybe we could make a boat out of *cassava*," the Rat suggested.

"What a good idea! Let's try it!"

It took some doing, but they finally had a craft that would float, and they

paddled off for all they were worth... but carefully! The water was roiling, and the current was swift. After a time, the Rat began to get tired and hungry. "Do you think I could just nibble of the tops off these *cassava* leaves at the rim of our boat?" she said to the Cat. "I've worked up quite an appetite."

"Are you out of your mind? Forget eating until we get ashore! Paddle, my friend! Paddle for your life!"

Night fell. The Cat, worn out from fighting the angry water, paused to rest. All at once, before she knew it, she had fallen asleep in the bottom of the boat. "Now's my chance!" thought the Rat. "I'll just munch a few of these leaves, and Friend Cat will be none the wiser." So she ate a leaf tip here and a stem there. Her appetite grew--the boat got smaller. Suddenly, it began to leak. In a matter of moments, even before the Cat came fully awake, the boat had sunk and both animals were swimming. By good luck they were near another hilltop, the very hilltop where they lived. After frantic effort, they were able to scramble up onto solid ground--wet, muddy and bedraggled, but alive and safe.

The Cat shook herself and looked at the Rat with eyes that burned like embers in a fire. "Hungry, were you?" she growled. "I feel like a snack, myself. I think I'll eat... *you*!"

"Eat *me*?" exclaimed the Rat, looking down at herself. "All muddy like this? You'll get grit in your teeth! Let me go clean up first!"

Leaving the Cat staring after her in startled fury, the Rat whisked right down her own hole which was not more than five jumps away. She didn't come out again, either... not until the Cat had given up waiting for her. Or maybe the Rat was able to change herself into a dog or a lion and walk right out under the nose of her former friend... because the Cat still keeps a sharp eye on every rat hole she comes across!

Afterword

Fables exist in every language and culture, in every age and epoch. They serve as guide posts along life's twisted path; they instruct and warn--they entertain. If they didn't, no one would remember them or heed their messages. The message partly concealed in most of these African fables is survival of the cleverest, pitted against superior physical or social forces.

Consider the humble trickster who wins out. He or she is a nuisance to the community, and yet is rewarded in the end. The sly, unscrupulous tortoise steals food, condemns an innocent monkey, and tricks a leopard into saving her life without even attempting to return the compliment. In masculine guise, the tortoise triumphs over a more honest but less resourceful rival in order to marry the daughter of the chief.

How can we condemn the opportunism of the Dog King's messenger when we laugh at the fruitless persistence of those who still search for him? Just as the hippos doubt the continued tolerance of the God of Land and Fire, we too, may secretly doubt the justice of "Powers That Be". Like the cassolo bird, we may also feel betrayed by those who do not wish us ill, yet will not save us in our time of need.

Equally fascinating for a different reason is the strange, composite tale of "The Serpent's Bride", which seems to include traditions from Western sources. We find the disobedient girl whose headstrong ways get her into trouble; the serpent as a symbol of evil, the many-headed Hydra of Hercules, subdued only by striking the true head, and the rescue effected by the teamwork of an unusual foursome: Carpenter, Hunter, Seer, and Thief.

Do all these factors have a common source? Who knows? Guinea-Bissau, where these fables were collected, was originally settled by tribespeople from eastern parts of the African continent. They may have brought these traditions with them from the eastern corner of the Mediterranean, while the same elements also simultaneously spread north and west to become a part of our own Western culture.

However that may be, this unusual little book, with its striking illustrations and memorable stories, gives us the opportunity today to enjoy some African culture.

--Feliz Guthrie